I SPY
Everything!

GOOD LUCK

I SPY with my little eye, something beginning with...

H is for

Hammer

I SPY with my little eye, something beginning with...

 **is for**

Van

I SPY with my little eye, something beginning with...

C is for

Cat

I SPY with my little eye, something beginning with...

D and E

D is for

Donut

E is for

Eggplant

I SPY with my little eye, something beginning with...

Q is for

Quail

I SPY with my little eye, something beginning with...

G

G _{is for}

Giraffe

I SPY with my little eye, something beginning with...

B

B is for Broccoli

I SPY with my little eye, something beginning with...

I and J

I is for

Ice cream cone

J is for

Jellyfish

I SPY with my little eye, something beginning with...

N

N is for

Nachos

I SPY with my little eye, something beginning with...

K

K is for

Ketchup

I SPY with my little eye, something beginning with...

S

S **is for**

Sailboat

I SPY with my little eye, something beginning with... O and P

O is for Octopus

P is for Peacock

I SPY with my little eye, something beginning with...

R

R is for

Rocket

I SPY with my little eye, something beginning with...

F

F is for

Fly

I SPY with my little eye, something beginning with...

A

A is for

Airplane

I SPY with my little eye, something beginning with...

T and U

T is for

Tacos

U is for

Urchin

I SPY with my little eye, something beginning with...

L is for

Lobster

I SPY with my little eye, something beginning with...

W

W is for

Worm

I SPY with my little eye, something beginning with...

M

M is for

Monster

I SPY with my little eye, something beginning with...
X, Y and Z

X is for

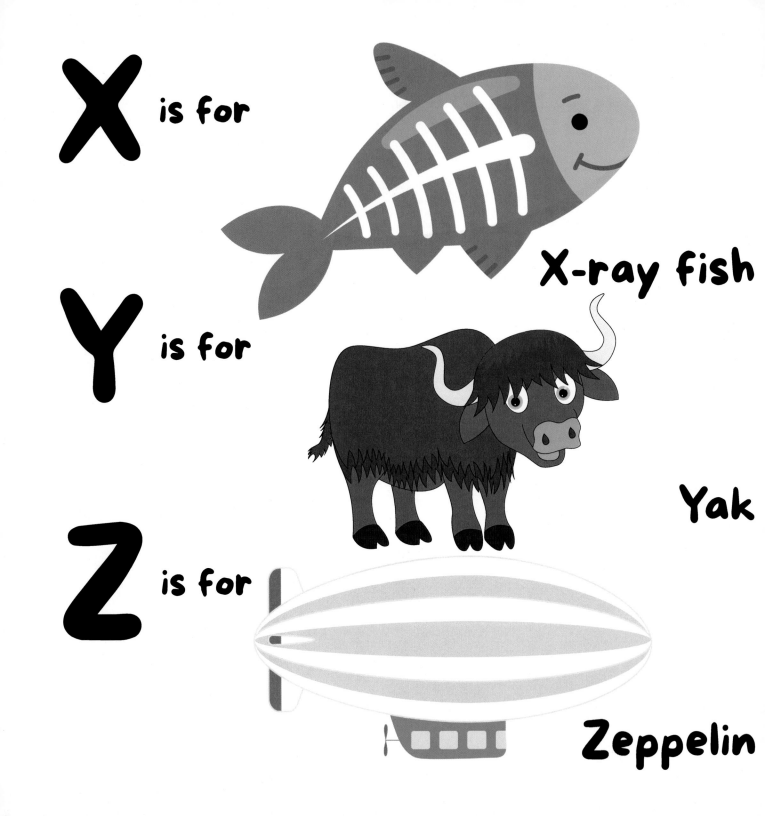

X-ray fish

Y is for

Yak

Z is for

Zeppelin

Made in the USA
Monee, IL
30 November 2021

83463112R00026